MAGICAL MOON

POEM OF LOVE

AUTHOR HEENA MARYAM

Contents

ABOUT THE BOOK

ABOUT THE BOOK

Magical Moon Poems for love brings together the greatest love
around the world through
ecstasy of passion,
Filled with verse that speaks to your heart, this anthology will
delight, comfort and inspire
anyone who has ever tasted love in any of its form.

ABOUT THE AUTHOR

AUTHOR BIO:-

Heena Maryam Khanum, magical moon capture the true essence of love in her poetry, She expresses So authentically her insight on love as she believes love to be many things least of all predictable. Love is beautiful and complicaled and breathtaking this is a book of poems that is an romance, loss and heartbreak, A voice for lover's, silent lovers, To all those who have loved and lost and keep on loving, despite it all. These Love poems are to no one. These love poems are to you.!!

Chapter1

SURVIVE

You fill my heart with joy,
You're my one and only hearts desire.
No matter what happens or what we go through,
I promise you that I'll stay beside you.

I simply don't know how?
Im thinking of you right now.
Im planning our future like I have a clue,
Don't know when will my dream come true.

I love the way we are together,
You can make smile just forever.
All these feelings I can't hide,
you're the reason I survive.

AUTHOR HEENA MARYAM

Chapter2

THROUGH THE STARS AND MOON
You are the blood that flows through me,
You are stars that glimmer oh so bright.
Meeting you has changed my life,
You can always make me smile.

All these feelings I just can't hide,
Now, my heart is filled with joy.
Like the birds flying high,
Nobody is as special as you are to me.

You have changed my life so much,
You make me happier than I have ever known.
Our love will continue till the heaven above,
Through the stars and moon above.

AUTHOR HEENA MARYAM

Chapter3

BE WITH ME

From staying strong to growning old,
From having fun to being in love.
From knowing you to knowing more,
From understanding you to understanding me.

From making you feel special to glowing look,
From being cold and being bold.
From knowing all to nothing know,
From reflections to walking alone.

From nothing to everything,
From everything to nothing.
From having you to having me,
All I need you is to be with me.

AUTHOR HEENA MARYAM

Chapter4

INTENTIONS
I need you there,
Always and forever.
Make you feel mine,
All I do is think of you.

Just like the shining magical moon,
I want our love to continue till end.
Not with the false intentions,
I want us to be pure.

I want us to be true.
Just like I want to marry you.
By making our life perfectly new.
AUTHOR HEENA MARYAM

Chapter5

REASON FOR LIVING

You're my reason for living,
My only reason to shine.
Just say you'll go with me,
Then, where, we'll decide.

Me without you,
is like a book without words.
I love the way you treat me,
And make me feel that im free.

I love you very much,
and don't want to let you go.
When I'm with you I'm in ecstasy,
Your embrace takes away all my problems and pain.

AUTHOR HEENA MARYAM

Chapter6

WHEN I FIRST MET YOU

When I first met you,
You were just a friend to me,
Now I can describe,
What you mean to me.

Things have changed between us,
Our friendship has changed into the relation,
My eyes always fear,
When your not so near.

When I text you I smile,
I feel happy to call you mine.
I know I can't see you everyday,
Just like the moon can't be with the sun.
AUTHOR HEENA MARYAM

Chapter7

FOR YOU I CAN

For you I can live this life,
For you I can leave this world.
For you I can do anything,
For you I can lie to things.

For you I would go through sleep,
For you I can fly miles.
For you I can kill the happiness,
For you I can fake the smile.

For you I can stop my tears,
For you I can carry all the fears.
For you I can die with peace,
For you and for you everything.
AUTHOR HEENA MARYAM

Chapter8

HARD TO HIDE

You're smile makes me shy,
Just like the clouds passes through the sky.
You're always here to make me cheer,
Just like a beautiful day without any fear.
I am the happiest person whenever you're near,
Sometimes I wonder where have you been all this time.
Since the day our conversations grew,
I became very fond of you.
The way I feel about you
can hardly be described,
what is harder still
is how hard it is to hide.

AUTHOR HEENA MARYAM

Chapter9

IM IN LOVE WITH YOU

There's no way to deny how I'm feeling inside,
I would make it so we were the way we were at the beginning.
You always know what to say,
Just talking to you can make my day.

The moment I think of you,
I go to another world.
You know what to say,
Just by reading my eyes and words.

People in your life will come and go,
But my love is true, and I'm sure you know.
So I'll say it how I feel it,
I'm in love with you.

AUTHOR HEENA MARYAM

Chapter10

REST OF MY LIFE

You are my one and only,
That comes to my eyes and mind.
You are the oxygen that keep's me alive,
You're so beautiful just like the sky.

My feelings for you is unstoppable,
My feeling for you is uncontrollable.
My feelings for you will never go,
like no one I have ever known.

Today, my heart is filled with joy,
You're always here to cheer me up so high.
You fill my heart with joy,
And with you I want to spend rest of my life.

AUTHOR HEENA MARYAM

Chapter11

WISH AND DREAM

For you, I would walk a thousand miles and more,
I will not have a future unless it involves you.
Your smile stops my world, even for a little while,
You always wipe away the tears I cry.
I'll express my love, so you know it's true,
There's nothing on earth, I would not do for you.
You are a gift greater than everything,
And for you, I'll do anything.
I enjoy every second I have sitting beside you,
You've filled my life with peaceful dreams.
You have given me the gift I seek,
Like the angels fulfil every wish and dream.

AUTHOR HEENA MARYAM

Chapter12

NEVER WANT TO LOSE YOU

We plan our future as if we have a clue,
I never want to lose you.
So, Love me and hold me tight,
as you tell me everything is all right.

I will never leave or give up on you,
I will always stay by your side.
I love the way we are together,
You can always make me smile.

I can't describe how much I care,
But when you need me, I'll be there.
Can't go a day without thinking about you,
No matter what happens or what we go through.

AUTHOR HEENA MARYAM

Chapter13

FOR YOU

For you I can cross the ocean,
For you I can Jump from the mountains.
For you I can walk on the streets,
For you I can leave all my dreams.

For you I can repeat all my sins,
For you I can give up on my dreams.
For you I can talk and scream,
For you I can leave my fears.

For you I can always wait,
Like you I can never create.
For you I can laugh like rain,
For you I can leave my tears.

AUTHOR HEENA MARYAM

Chapter14

LOST SMILE

I found the smile I thought I had lost,
I hope this relationship gets really far.
We will always be strong together....you made me realize who I really am,
Under the stars at night.

Me and you
Have been through a lot,
No matter how much we fight,
Things will be okay.

Since the day i met you,
I became very fond of you.
So many things I love about you, it's hard to name them all.

AUTHOR HEENA MARYAM

Chapter15

INCOMPLETE WITHOUT YOU

Love is what makes us so special,
Trust, Support, Understanding and True.
Dream of the blessed day when together we shall be,
Like the rainbow looking at sky, just like you look into me.

I shall owe you to show the paradise and the beautiful sky,
Nothing is more beautiful than your smile.
My heart beats fast, when I look at your deep eyes,
With the beautiful love which is hidden inside.

Your the sky, which completes the beautiful moon and stars and sun and lights.
Like the ocean in which I can survive,
Like nobody else can fly so high.
Incomplete without you,
Without the future (You).
Without your smile,
Without ur eyes.

AUTHOR HEENA MARYAM

Printed by Libri Plureos GmbH in Hamburg,
Germany